T0067090

LITTLE SPIRIT Spark

PEGGY DAVINE

BALBOA.
PRESS

A DIVISION OF HAY HOUSE

Balboa Press books may be ordered through
booksellers or by contacting:

Balboa Press
A Division of Hay House
1663 Liberty Drive
Bloomington, IN 47403
www.balboapress.com
1 (877) 407-4847

Because of the dynamic nature of the Internet, any web
addresses or links contained in this book may have changed
since publication and may no longer be valid. The views
expressed in this work are solely those of the author and do
not necessarily reflect the views of the publisher, and the
publisher hereby disclaims any responsibility for them.

The author of this book does not dispense medical advice or prescribe
the use of any technique as a form of treatment for physical, emotional,
or medical problems without the advice of a physician, either directly
or indirectly. The intent of the author is only to offer information
of a general nature to help you in your quest for emotional and
spiritual well-being. In the event you use any of the information
in this book for yourself, which is your constitutional right, the
author and the publisher assume no responsibility for your actions.

Any people depicted in stock imagery provided by Thinkstock are
models, and such images are being used for illustrative purposes only.
Certain stock imagery © Thinkstock.

Print information available on the last page.

ISBN: 978-1-5043-2809-8 (sc)
ISBN: 978-1-5043-2810-4 (e)

Balboa Press rev. date: 03/27/2015

Foreword

Many have wondered where they came from, who they are, their purpose, and what happens after this. Many have consciously studied, traveled, meditated, and contemplated the meaning of Life. Along the way, here and there, they have garnered bits of Truth. Now, in our time, we must gather all the bits together so we have the whole picture.

Little Spirit Spark's story is everyone's story. Just like Little Spirit Spark, each one of us has been prepared for life on Earth. Buddha remembered. Jesus remembered. There have been others. But humanity as a whole, chose to ignore the Creator's Plan. Now it is time for all of us to remember who we are, where we came from, and our purpose.

Due to the need of the hour, we are being given assistance from the Realms of Light never before allowed. Truth is all around us. We must listen with our heart to discern it.

Chapter One

Once upon a time long, long ago, there lived a Little Spirit Spark. He was a newly born Spark from the Creator of All That Is. He knew himself as an individual "I AM" consciousness--free to create as his Creator did.

He lived in a land of Boundless Splendor and Infinite Light. The atmosphere was alive with the sounds of creation. Shining Angels and Archangels of all colors and hues radiated their own special quality given them by the Creator of All That Is. Ascended Masters shone with the dignity of a Christ. Mighty Elohim and beautiful Devas and elementals were creating Planets and Stars and moving the Cosmos.

Mighty Seraphim passed by, their great Light spreading out behind them like a fan and looking very much like a shooting star. Wherever they appeared, glorious music could be heard.

Anyone traveling in a Seraphim's Light would safely arrive at their destination. It could be a group of Great Advanced Beings on their way to a cosmic gathering. It could be a happy group of volunteers on their way to create a new universe. Whoever it was, a Great Seraphim and His merry followers were a marvelous sight.

Everyone could travel safely to other planets, universes, and galaxies when the Cosmic Highways were open. This was a joyous time of friends meeting friends as they passed one another on their way to explore more of the Creator's Land of Boundless Splendor and Infinite Light. Always there was music, beauty, and perfection. Little Spirit Spark made sure he returned to his starting point before the Cosmic Highways were closed.

He enjoyed being an individual "I AM" conscious Being. He could flit about and investigate anything that caught his attention. He was doing just that when his attention was drawn to a beautiful Deva poised gracefully above a newly formed planet. She was adding the final touches to make it beautiful for Light Beings wishing to use the planet to develop and expand the use of their individual powers of creation.

Suddenly, he felt a desire to create something beautiful of his own. So calling his "I AM" Presence to guide his thought and feeling, he created an exact copy of one of the Deva's flame flowers.

Slowly he began to create his own flame flowers; then, tiny cherubim and small temples. To his delight, the more he used his "I AM" consciousness, the more confident he became. Everything he created was perfect for all he saw was perfect. He began to send his creations out into his world.

The more he created, the stronger his Spark became. As his Spark developed into a powerful flame, its Light expanded all around him. When his flame became still and calm and unwavering, its Light expanded even more. He was developing into a strong Being of Light.

From the very beginning of his birth as an "I AM" conscious being, all his experiences in the Realms of Light were recorded in his Causal Body. All the Good he created was there for all to see.

Nobody knows how long he stayed in this blissful state for in the Land of Boundless Splendor and Infinite Light there is no such thing as time.

Many have chosen to always live in this realm of perfection. But Little Spirit Spark was one of the brave spirits who wanted to experiment with Life in its fullness. He wished to develop greater dexterity in drawing the powers of creation through his thought and feeling centers.

As he became conscious of this desire, immediately stretched out before him were seven magnificent and perfect Spheres. In each Sphere the vibration of the electronic building substance became slower. The slower the electronic substance, the more effort it took to make perfect creations.

This was just what Little Spirit Spark wished to experience. Other Spirit Sparks also wished to expand their experiment with Life, and so together they slowly entered into the first Sphere of Light.

Chapter Two

The First Sphere

*I*n the First Sphere he found other "I AM" flames already there. They were drawing the Divine Ideas of the Creator of All That Is into this slower vibration and then projecting those ideas outward to the next Sphere.

This First Sphere was not so very different from his homeland and he adjusted quickly. Using his individual creative abilities of thought and feeling, and guided by his "I AM" Presence, he drew the Power and Will of the Creator into this Sphere. Then he directed this Power and Will out to the next Sphere. The vibration of Divine Power and Will is seen as the color blue. So a blue band of Light was added to his Causal Body.

When he felt ready, Little Spirit Spark joined the more adventurous who were ready to move into the next Sphere. Some chose to remain in this Sphere and go no further.

The Second Sphere

In the Second Sphere dwelt very advanced Spirits busy receiving the qualities from the First Sphere and molding them into thoughts. Here he anchored the Wisdom of the Creator and sent it out to the next Sphere. The vibration of Divine Wisdom is seen as the color yellow. Thus he built the color yellow into his Causal Body.

When he felt ready, Little Spirit Spark and the more adventurous moved on into the third Sphere. Some chose to remain here and go no further.

The Third Sphere

In the Third Sphere, Little Spirit Spark joined the many great Beings already there. They were known as the embodied representatives of Holy Spirit. The activity of Holy Spirit is to breathe the Love of the Creator of All That Is into the perfect forms from the Second Sphere, energizing them with perfect feeling so they became Living Beings. Then he projected them out to the next Realm.

As he worked, he was filled with all the qualities of Divine Love. The vibration of Divine Love is the color pink. Thus he built the color pink into his Causal Body.

As he worked alongside the great Masters in this Sphere, he became aware that in the Realms below, he could create beautiful forms that would be useful to anyone living on a planet.

When he was ready, Little Spirit Spark moved on. Some chose to stay in this beautiful Sphere of Love and go no further.

The Fourth Sphere

In the Fourth Sphere magnificent Brothers and Sisters were tuning into their own "I AM" Presence and were creating beautiful paintings, buildings, ideas for poetry, heavenly music, and other works of art. Little Spirit Spark especially enjoyed the music and would go from one music temple to another learning about all the different musical instruments. There were temples where the mathematics of vibration and sound were explored.

In one of the temples, on a high dais, stood an especially grand organ made of something that looked like shining crystal. The keyboards were made of iridescent mother-of-pearl and the pipes were made of glowing gold. How happy he was when he played this organ.

His music wafted through the air and became a part of the celestial music all around. He learned to direct his music into the next lower Sphere. Anyone in the next Sphere who was interested could pick up the music and anchor it into that lower vibration.

Oh what a joy it was. He stayed in this vibration longer than any other, thus adding a broad band of white to his Causal Body.

However, when he felt he was ready, he continued his adventure. Some chose to stay in this Sphere and go no further.

The Fifth Sphere

He moved on to the Fifth Sphere and there he saw the beautiful Temple of Truth. Also in this Sphere were Temples of Consecration and Concentration. Here he explored the secrets of nature. The Light Beings who dwell in this Sphere are known as a Guardian Presence to those who devote their lives to the use of science, formulas, and many healing methods.

While in this Sphere, Little Spirit Spark decided he would use music to bless all life. He chose to build an organ to add to his mastery of his favorite instrument.

Using his knowledge of mathematics and scientific understanding, Little Spirit Spark concentrated on the sounds and vibrations that would best express the Beauty, Love, and Healing of the Creator of All That Is. So asking his Mighty "I AM" Presence to guide and direct him, Little Spirit Spark built an organ from the primal energy of this Sphere. Then he directed these instructions out to the next lower Sphere.

The healing vibration is green. So a green band of Light was added to his Causal Body. Many remain within this Sphere, finding such happiness and joy they go no further. Little Spirit Spark moved on.

The Sixth Sphere

In the Sixth Sphere, he found Brothers and Sisters who anchored the Spirit of the Creator's nature. The Love of the Creator in this Sphere is expressed as Reverence, Devotion, and Worship. Here he learned the power of service to others. In this Sphere he anchored the quality of gratitude for Life itself.

How grateful he was to his "I AM" Presence and the Creator of All That Is for the Peace and Contentment he was anchoring into this Sphere. All he learned, he sent out to the next Sphere. And so it was that the rose color was added to his Causal Body.

Many remain in this Sphere and go no further. When he felt he was ready, Little Spirit Spark entered the Seventh, and last Sphere.

The Seventh Sphere

In the Seventh Sphere he used all he had learned in all the other Spheres. Little Spirit Spark experimented with Divine Alchemy. From the Light Beings already in this Sphere, he learned the powers of the Violet Fire. He was filled with Mercy, Love, and Compassion until he became Mercy, Love, and Compassion. He learned to balance Power with Love until he was Wisdom itself. He learned that rhythmic action in the lower vibrational world of form resulted in lasting perfect results. He directed the Angels of Mercy into the world of form. He was building a violet band into his Causal Body.

When he had completed his sojourn in this Violet Sphere, he had all the energy, knowledge and gifts of the Creator that he would ever need to successfully embody on a planet. Now, wherever he went, his seven planetary bands of color shone brightly in his Causal Body.

Chapter Three

*L*ittle Spirit Spark was very interested in all of Creation. So of course he chose to embody. He lived on many different planets in many different solar systems in many different universes. Life on each planet was different. Yet each one was perfect. That was because Life on each planet was fulfilling its purpose perfectly. All was held in the Harmony, Peace, and Love of the Creator.

Wherever he went he added his own perfect creations and was known by all the good he had accumulated in his Causal Body. Little Spirit Spark had developed into a Being of Great Light.

He was on the Planet Venus when the Great Divine Fiat was declared. This was the Great Call--the Great Summons-- that all of Creation had been waiting to hear for eons.

The Fiat went out throughout the firmament, calling all Spirit Sparks to return to the Creator of All That Is. A wonderful stir was felt through every planet, solar system, universe, and galaxy. All Life everywhere began to hum with anticipation of moving up in vibration and closer to the Creator.

All was in readiness except one small planet called Earth. It no longer emitted enough Light to fulfill its Divine Plan. Great Beings from Great Stars had left their perfect realms of Light, took on a physical body, and brought the message of Truth to Earth. Great Golden Ages were created, but when these Great Beings left the Earth plane, the people began to misinterpret these messages of Truth and again created imperfection. In the Realms of Light, Earth was known as "the Dark Star."

The Cosmos could no longer wait for Earth. The Creator, out of Love for all his creation, could no longer allow Life to be delayed by this one small wayward planet. So, the long awaited Fiat had come forth declaring it was time to begin the journey back to their Creator and share their harvest of achievements. All those who were ready would move closer to the Creator.

A call went out asking for a final effort to save Earth. Volunteers from many Perfect Realms of Light again came before the Great Wise Ones to offer their service to Earth. This was Earth's last opportunity to awaken.

Little Spirit Spark wanted to help Earth. He knew his knowledge of vibration and sound could reach that tiny flame still flickering in each heart of Earth's humanity. This could assist in opening their hearts to the Truth of who they truly are. So it was, that the Great Light Being we call Little Spirit Spark, was one of the many volunteers to go before the Great Wise Ones and humbly ask for the opportunity to go to Earth.

All of the volunteers who went before the Great Wise Ones were shown a cosmic screen which showed the story of Earth as it was when the Elohim first created her.

The Earth as it was in the Beginning

In the beginning, seven great Elohim agreed to use their powers of Thought and Feeling to create a shining Orb of Light. They stood in a circle and projected a Ray of Light into the center and where these seven Rays of Light came together, a Flame of Life blazed forth.

Two Mighty Beings volunteered to hold this Flame and keep it balanced and unchanging for as long as it was needed. Around this flame, a new planet was created. This Flame in the center of Earth was called The Sun of Even Pressure and could be seen sending forth a radiation that was visible as a soft glow beneath the grass, flowers, and the oceans.

Beloved Amaryllis, Neptune, Aries, Devas of all orders, and all the Beings of Nature had volunteered to add their gifts of perfection to this beautiful Orb. All the temples radiated a soft light and the flowers were so alive they were called flame flowers. The grass was always the perfect height, the mountains were magnificent, and the rivers were sparkling Light. There was no decay. They created such a perfect planet that when mankind first embodied upon it, there was little difference between the Earth and the Seven Spheres.

When the Earth was ready, the Mighty Lord, Archangel Michael Himself, led shining Light Beings using the "I AM" consciousness down to Earth to expand their Service to the Light. They walked and talked with the Angels and Great Masters.

From their own Individual "I AM" Presence they received the Will of the Creator in the form of ideas. Using dear elementals, who had volunteered to outpicture whatever the "I AM" conscious beings chose to create, they molded beautiful forms and then filled these forms with the feeling of Love. They created on Earth just as they had created in the Realms of Light.

Beautiful gifts were added to Earth and many Spirit Sparks completed the course of evolution in perfect harmony and returned to the Realms of Light.

Then the Cosmic Screen grew dark and the Volunteers were shown why Earth could not return to the Realms of Light.

What Happened

A few souls on Earth chose to use the Freedom they had been given by the Creator of All That Is, to misuse Life Energy. Other Spirit Sparks also experimented in the use of lower vibrations not in the Original Divine

Plan. Their creations were not pure and could not return to the perfect Realms of Light.

These imperfect creations had no place to go so they began to gather in the atmosphere of Earth and form shadows. These shadows grew so dense the Spirit Sparks began to forget their connection with the Realms of Light. They were creating suffering, disease, and decay. They took on dense physical bodies and were called hu-mans.

They no longer remembered their Mighty "I AM" Presence and could not find their way out of the shadows they had created.

In Mercy, to ease the pain and suffering, the Creator of All That Is reduced the power of their flame. Now, all that sustained them was a small flicker of the Creator's Light anchored in their heart. Yet that small flame was pure and held the desire to find "something better." But no matter where or how hu-mans searched, they could not find that "something better."

They were lost and struggling in the darkness they themselves had created. This was not the wonderful Life the Creator had planned for his children.

When the Cosmic Screen closed, all the volunteers were even more desirous of helping Earth and its people.

The Great Wise Ones had the enormous task of choosing those volunteers whose achievements best fitted the need of the hour. The Earth had so very much "catching up" to do.

The Great Wise Ones looked carefully and thoughtfully at the achievements of each volunteer. When Little Spirit Spark was called, the Great Wise Ones looked at his experiences built into his Causal Body.

*They saw the strength of
his devotion to Life and
the Love he radiated.

*They saw his powerful desire
to expand the Will of the
Creator to raise the planet and
its people into the Light.

*He had a strong understanding
of the Truths of Creation.

*He loved Life deeply enough
to withstand the dark shadows
weighing so heavily on Earth.

*He could hold the purity
of his mission and draw only

the perfection and beauty of
his Mighty "I AM" Presence
into Earth and its people.

*He could use his music and
understanding of vibration
and sound to raise the
vibration of Life on Earth.

*He could hold his own peace,
harmony, and balance, so that
his Mighty "I AM" Presence
flowed through his every thought,
feeling, word, and action.

*He could, in an orderly
fashion, focus on his plan
so as to be successful.

        *He could use the Violet
Fire to transmute the
shadows back into Light.

The Great Wise Ones said, "You have passed through the Seven Spheres of Learning. You have experienced all the wonderful creations that are waiting to manifest on the earth. You know the beauty of the earth as it was in the beginning and as it was meant to be. At your request, we now give you liberty to use your creative abilities of thought and feeling as you see fit to recreate the beautiful perfect ideas intended for earth in the beginning. You will be summoned when an appropriate earth body presents itself."

Little Spirit Spark was filled with joy. He had been chosen! He was so grateful for the opportunity to assist in raising the vibration of Earth and its' people so they could continue with their solar system. He was taken to a magnificent temple set aside for those waiting for a physical body. While he waited to be summoned, he continued to prepare. He was well aware that once he stepped through the Veil of Forgetfulness he would forget the perfect Realms of Light.

The Summons

A beautiful shining Angel came with the news that an earth body had become available. The Angel accompanied him to this very solemn ceremony. Cosmic energy and planetary conditions must line up with mathematical precision for the delicate transfer of consciousness from the Spheres of Light into the dense, lower vibrations of Earth.

Beautiful shining Angels trained especially for this ceremony accompanied each volunteer to their special seat in the Great Hall. They stood beside each volunteer until everyone who had come to participate in the ceremony had arrived.

When all was ready, the music of an Angelic Choir filled the Great Hall announcing the arrival of the Great Wise Ones. Everyone stood in recognition of the great achievements and awesome responsibility these Great Wise Ones had accepted.

They were clothed in magnificent robes of Light and for this ceremony each one had created a beautiful jewel which was attached to a golden chain around the neck. The jewel rested on the heart and the color of the jewel represented the Ray on which each of them served. It was a majestic procession as they made their way to the center of the Great Hall. The Love they radiated could be felt by everyone. They took their places and the ceremony began.

It is a deep Love of Life that brings an "I AM" Conscious Being to leave the glories of the Land of Boundless Splendor and Infinite Light and take on a heavy human form.

Everyone knew that Little Spirit Spark and all the volunteers would forget the Realms of Light and who they truly are. He would have to find his way through the dense shadows of Earth, remember he was a Spark direct from The Creator of All That Is, and complete his mission. Only on completion of his service to Earth while in his physical body could he again ascend to the Realms of Light.

He, and all the other "I AM" conscious beings who were receiving a physical body, joined the Great Wise Ones to receive their final blessing. One of the Great Wise Ones was the Goddess of Liberty. The last consciousness in the Realms of Light was filled with Her words:

"You are at liberty Beloved, to take pure and primal Life into the earth plane. You are at liberty in the outer (physical appearance world) to use Life as you choose. You are at liberty Beloved, to call upon any and all of us as you may choose, to assist you when the momentums and energies of your world seem not sufficient to handle the conditions or to radiate the Life to fulfill your divine plan. You have to accept the Flame of Liberty which I AM endowed to pass through the lifestream, before opportunity to embody is given. So is the flame woven into the essence of the heart beat. Only to these is given opportunity to embody."

At the precise cosmic moment, Little Spirit Spark stepped through the Veil of Forgetfulness and was gone.

Chapter Four

The Earth Plane

*L*ittle Spirit Spark awoke to a harsh bright light. Physical bodies in white uniforms were all around him. He heard a loud, frightened cry. It was coming from himself! He tried to speak but all he could do was that loud cry. His arms and legs kept flailing about in jerky movements and did not do what he wanted them to do. Then he felt warm loving arms about him and he relaxed and fell asleep. The loving arms belonged to his earth mother.

When he opened his eyes again, he was wrapped in soft blankets and lying on his back. He could not move. His body felt wet. He wanted to ask someone to explain the situation, but all he could do was that loud frightened cry.

He soon realized that everyone expected him to cry and even seemed pleased, because every time he cried out, someone immediately came to care for him.

At first he was very busy learning to use his arms and legs. With encouragement, he learned to roll over and sit up. He learned to stretch out his arms and pick up toys with his five fingers. He learned to pull himself up to a standing position. He had to move around on his hands and knees before he could balance on his feet and walk like other hu-mans. And during all this, he was learning to use his vocal chords and mouth to shape sounds that helped him communicate with other hu-mans. And he had to eat something called food. At first someone had to feed him. But he learned to hold a spoon and feed himself. He was messy at first because he kept missing his mouth.

Adjusting to a physical body really did take more energy. It took great effort, thought, and determination.

He was so focused on learning earth "things," that he did not notice he had forgotten who he was and where he had come from. But as hu-man babies do, he gained control of his body and learned to talk. He repeated sounds over and over until he was understood by others. He learned to move his hands, arms, and legs so he could stay on top of water. It was called swimming. He learned to ride a bicycle.

He liked school very much. He played different kinds of ball games, but his favorites were tennis and baseball. He learned that hu-mans living on another part of the Earth used different sounds to say the same thing. So he chose to learn French and German in school so he could talk to people from other countries. He was taught about the universe as it was understood on Earth. History was a subject in school that seemed to be mostly about how hu-mans caused great harm to themselves and to the Earth.

But there were wonderful things too. Museums were filled with beautiful paintings, and there were tall stone and brick buildings, airplanes, electricity, boats, and vast fields of flowers and vegetables.

He especially loved music. He took piano lessons and sang in the church choir. When he was 12 years old, his mother and father took him to the big city to attend his first musical concert. It was held in a grand cathedral with soaring ceilings and arches, and a large organ with many pipes. There were so many pipes, some had to be along the walls of the cathedral and some were in the basement.

After the concert, there was a tour of the cathedral and that included a close look at the organ. Little Spirit Spark listened carefully when the organist explained about the bellows that pumped air and the leather and little round knobs on each side that you pulled out and pushed in. The organ had three keyboards. There were wooden pedals near the floor that were played with the feet! It was like dancing. Not only did the organ have its own sound, but it could make the sound of the violin, the trumpet, bells, harp, even deep thunder sounds. What a wonderful instrument!

Oh this he had to learn to play. His mother and father were pleased to have a child so interested in music. So they went to a church in a bigger town nearby that had an organ.

The organ master was a very nice man and he agreed to teach Little Spirit Spark how to play. He even gave Little Spirit Spark permission to use the church organ to practice when the organ was not in use. Little Spirit Spark was such a good pupil, he was asked to play for the church services whenever the organ master was away.

He finished high school and attended a music college. He was a dedicated student and when offered the opportunity, Little Spirit Spark entered musical contests and competitions and gave concerts. He began to compose his own musical pieces. Word of his accomplishments became known and he was asked to play in the surrounding towns and cities.

After completing his college training, he began to travel to other countries. His knowledge of three languages came in handy. Many of his concerts were in beautiful cathedrals for that was where the grand organs were. He enjoyed the beautiful statues and stained-glass windows in these majestic buildings of worship. The beautifully carved wood pews were polished from centuries of use and loving care.

The dream

It was on a concert tour in Europe that he had a dream. It seemed so real. In his dream he was in a great open space filled with Light. He was seated at a magnificent organ whose pipes were gold and reached high into the atmosphere. As he played this wonderful instrument, shining Beings of Light began to gather around him. It was all so joyful and harmonious. When he woke from the dream, he wondered what it meant. But he had no time to think about it because he had to be on his way to his next concert engagement.

A few weeks later, he had another dream. In this dream, he was in a huge amphitheater in the atmosphere above Earth. There was an organ in the center of the amphitheater made of a glowing substance. He wore a white garment and his body felt light.

An invisible power moved him to the organ and he began playing. As he played the organ, beautiful shining Beings in white garments like his, came and filled the atmosphere. All around him they gathered. Tier after tier into the atmosphere they gathered, filling everything with their Light. The Light expanded throughout the amphitheater and beyond until it completely enfolded all Life in, on, and around the Earth. Little Spirit Spark was filled to overflowing with Love and Comforting Peace. He awoke still feeling the Light, the majesty, and the wonder of it all.

Little Spirit Spark finished his concert tour and returned home. At a concert a few months later, he was playing one of his favorite compositions when a beautiful orb of Light appeared in the air in front of the organ. Within that Light a beautiful Angel appeared. The Angel and its Light moved through the air until it was standing above the audience. Then the Angel expanded its Light until it filled the concert hall and passed through the walls and into the surrounding area beyond.

Little Spirit Spark looked quickly at the people and could tell they did not see the Angel. As the Light faded away, his physical body felt light and peaceful. Everything was effortless; his fingers seemed to move over the keyboard by themselves. He wasn't even thinking about the piece he was playing yet he knew the music continued. Somehow he finished the concert and went home to think about the meaning of these magnificent dreams and his vision.

As the days passed, he began to remember the Realms of Light. He remembered the Angels. He remembered the Great Wise Ones. He remembered his "I AM" Presence. He remembered he was a Light Being direct from The Creator of All That Is. He remembered why he was in a physical earth body.

As he continued to draw the memory of who he really was into his physical brain, he began consciously sending his Love and Gratitude to his Mighty "I AM" Presence. He now understood he had been guided to study music so he would be prepared to fulfill his mission on the earth plane.

Every day he drew into his physical body the memories of who he really was. Now he could consciously cooperate with his Mighty "I AM" Presence and asked his Presence to guide and direct him. He called for the perfection of the Realms of Light to flow through him and into the earth plane. He called the shining Angels to come and radiate their Light into all Life on Earth. What joy! He was so very grateful to have remembered who he really was and that his body could be used to anchor the Light of the Creator of All That Is into the earth plane.

The concerts gave him the opportunity to serve many, many people. Before each concert he now called his Mighty "I AM" Presence to blaze Its Perfect Light through him and his music and bless those who were in the audience. He called the Angels to come and radiate their particular gifts of the Creator into each individual, raising everyone up in energy, vibration, and consciousness.

Every concert sparkled with Light for Little Spirit Spark was in touch with the perfection of his real home. Everywhere people came to hear him and were lifted out of their ordinary daily experiences and into a wonderful feeling of calm, comfort, confidence, and well-being.

As they listened to the organ music, the worried brow, the tight stooped shoulders gave way to a relaxed face, a smile, and they seemed to sit a little straighter. As they left the concert, they smiled and nodded a greeting to each other.

Little Spirit Spark always remembered to send Love and Gratitude to his Mighty "I AM" Presence. Each day, from his Mighty "I AM" Presence, he called the Violet Fire from the Realms of Light to transmute hu-manity's misconceptions, imperfect thoughts and feelings, and directed that purified energy to return to the Realms of Light. He called the Angels to blaze their Light in, on, and around the Earth and its people.

Chapter Five

As the years passed by, his earth body began to change. It was not as strong; his hair lost its color. He no longer made the long trips to other countries. But his compassion for Earth, its hu-manity, and all Life associated with Earth, grew stronger.

He had faithfully followed the Truth of who he was to the best of his understanding. He was so grateful for the protection and guidance of his Mighty "I AM" Presence and for the assistance of the Angels and other Light Beings.

He had seen music cut right through the limited ideas and misconceptions of hu-manity and open their hearts to the Love vibrations of the Angels. He had seen the loving vibrations and sounds of music heal in hospitals. He had seen compassionate direction of musical tones dispel grief. Wherever he traveled, he saw music lift the Spirit when life on Earth seemed too heavy to bear.

He always sent his Love and appreciation to his Mighty "I AM" Presence and to the Angels and Light Beings who responded immediately when he called for Their assistance. He had indeed remembered his purpose and he was content.

Leaving the Earth Plane

As Little Spirit Spark's allotted time on the "Dark Star" came to an end, he called his earth family and close friends together to thank them for their Love and support during his journey on Earth. He reminded them to send gratitude and Love to their own Mighty "I AM" Presence for the gift of Life and the opportunity they had to serve the Light while they were on Earth.

As Cosmic Holy Spirit received his last breath, Little Spirit Spark could feel himself zooming towards a pin point of white Light. Yet he did not feel any wind or movement. The heaviness of the earth body melted away.

As he got near the point of Light, it opened up to reveal the glorious, perfect Land of Boundless Splendor and Infinite Light. As he adjusted to the Light, he could see the Great Wise Ones and Beings of Light enfolding him in their magnificent loving Light waiting to greet him. "Welcome home Beloved. You broke through the Veil of Forgetfulness and fulfilled your purpose. Welcome home!" There was great rejoicing all around for one of the Creator's children had returned.

Beautiful Angels came and lovingly guided him to a Glorious Temple especially set aside for those returning from the lower vibrations of Earth. A quiet room with a soft bed of rose petals had been made ready for him. While he rested, he remembered Earth and its struggling hu-manity. He knew he would volunteer to go again.

When he was adjusted to his Light Body, he went directly to the temple with the beautiful sparkling crystal organ and glowing golden pipes that reached high into the atmosphere. He played a hymn of Gratitude and Praise to his Mighty "I AM" Presence and the Creator of All That Is for the opportunity to serve Earth and its people. As the music wafted through the heavens, everyone heard it, and smiled.

Little Spirit Spark was home.

Acknowledgments

I send love and gratitude to my
own Mighty "IAM" Presence
and those of all humanity, the
Ascended Masters, the Beloved
Angelic Kingdom, the Beloved
Elemental Kingdom, and
all the Great Cosmic Beings
for their love and assistance
to Earth and its people.

The quote of the Great Wise
Ones and the quote of the

Goddess of Liberty were taken from "Law of Life and Teachings by Divine Beings" by A. D. K. Luk. The description of the Realms of Light are found in many writings, but, for this story, the approach of A.D.K. Luk was chosen. I am very grateful.

To all the dear ones who expressed an interest in my book, I thank you. You warmed my heart and encouraged me more than you know.